The Biography of Sir Karl Jenkins

The Fascinating Journey of The Man Who Was
Mistaken As Meghan Markle at the Coronation, His
Legacy And Impact

Robert C. Rameriz

Table of Content

Introduction

Sir Karl Jenkins is a composer, performer, and conductor who has had a considerable effect on the music business throughout the course of his lengthy career. From his early days as a jazz and jazz-rock musician to his transition into classical music and his exploration of world music and cultural fusion, Jenkins has demonstrated an unwavering commitment to pushing the boundaries of musical expression and creating works that resonate with audiences around the world.

In this book, we will go into the life and work of Sir Karl Jenkins, studying his early inspirations, his creative progress, and his contributions to numerous genres of music. We will analyze the evolution of his distinctive style and his approach to composition and consider some of his most prominent pieces, including Adiemus, Requiem, and The Armed Man: A Mass for Peace.

We will also analyze Jenkins' effect on the music business and his ongoing legacy, which stretches well beyond his contributions to music. We will read about his charitable endeavors and his social engagement, including his participation with groups such as the British Red Cross, Cancer Research UK, and the Prince's Trust.

We hope that this book will encourage readers to expand their awareness of Jenkins' work and its larger cultural relevance and to explore the various layers of his distinctive aesthetic vision.

Chapter 1: Early Life, Education and Career

Sir Karl Jenkins was born in Penclawdd, a tiny hamlet in Wales, on February 17th, 1944. He grew up in a musical household, with his mother being a pianist and his father playing the euphonium.

Jenkins' parents noticed his musical skills at an early age and pushed him to pursue music. He began taking piano lessons when he was five years old and subsequently started playing the oboe and saxophone.

Jenkins' early musical inspirations were eclectic, and he was exposed to a wide spectrum of genres, from classical to jazz. He has identified the works of Bach, Stravinsky, and Bartók as early inspirations, as well as jazz superstars like Miles Davis and John Coltrane.

His interest in jazz and jazz-rock was aroused by the music of the Dave Brubeck Quartet and the saxophonist Paul Desmond. Jenkins' schooling and training as a musician started at the Cardiff University School of Music, where he studied composition under Alun Hoddinott and got a degree in music.

He subsequently went on to pursue additional studies at the Royal Academy of Music in London, where he studied oboe under Terence MacDonagh and composition with John Lambert.

Jenkins' early career was distinguished by his engagement in the jazz and jazz-rock genres. He performed with numerous renowned ensembles, including the Graham Collier Sextet, the Don Rendell-Ian Carr Quintet, and Nucleus. During this period, he also started to explore his own compositions, infusing aspects of jazz into his music.

In 1970, Jenkins established the jazz-rock ensemble Soft Machine with Hugh Hopper, Mike Ratledge, and Robert Wyatt. He played saxophone, oboe, and keyboards with the band and contributed to many of their albums, including Third and Fourth.

Soft Machine established a dedicated fanbase in the UK and worldwide, and their music had a huge effect on the jazz and rock cultures of the period.

Despite the success of his jazz and jazz-rock careers, Jenkins started to feel pulled towards classical music and chose to turn his concentration towards composing. He started training under the composer Sir William Walton and went on to engage with some of the best classical performers and ensembles of the day, including the London Philharmonic Orchestra and the City of Birmingham Symphony Orchestra.

Jenkins' early pieces in the classical genre were defined by his exploration of form, texture, and tone. He mixed elements of jazz, rock, and classical music to develop a distinct sound that would come to characterize his subsequent work.As Jenkins' passion for classical music expanded, he became more intrigued by the concept of adding world music elements to his songs.

He thought that Western classical music had become too insular and confined in its breadth and that by incorporating aspects from other cultures, he might create a more wide and inclusive musical language.

Jenkins started to travel widely, visiting places such as India, Indonesia, and Japan to study their music and learn about their cultures. He also investigated African music and grew especially interested in the music of South Africa, which would eventually have a key influence on his work.

Jenkins' early classical works were noted for their inventive use of percussion and orchestration, as well as their inclusion of non-Western musical influences. His first significant work in this genre was the 1974 composition "Sinfonia for Strings," which was debuted by the London Philharmonic Orchestra.

In 1980, Jenkins co-founded the Adiemus Project, a vocal group that would become one of his most well-known and lasting musical works. The group's unusual style, which merged Western classical music with African and other world music elements, earned them an immediate sensation and helped cement Jenkins' image as a composer who was willing to take chances and explore new musical territories.

Over the course of his career, Jenkins has continued to push the frontiers of musical expression, exploring a broad variety of genres and styles and working with musicians from varied ethnic backgrounds.

He has created operas, ballets, film soundtracks, and music for television, as well as many pieces for choir, orchestra, and chamber groups.

Through it all, Jenkins has stayed devoted to producing music that is both original and accessible and that speaks to the human experience in all its complexity and variety. His distinctive aesthetic vision and his passion for his craft have made him one of the most important and beloved composers of our time, and his imprint on the world of music is set to remain for years to come.

Jenkins' early classical pieces, including "Sinfonia for Strings," were widely lauded for their inventiveness and unique use of tonality, as well as their use of non-Western musical influences. These paintings represented the beginning of Jenkins' experimentation with new forms and methods, which would continue throughout his career.

In the 1990s, Jenkins started to investigate the notion of producing a piece that would merge classical and world music components in a manner that had never been done before. The result was his best-known tune, "Adiemus," which was initially published in 1995 as part of the album "Songs of Sanctuary."

Overall, Sir Karl Jenkins' early upbringing and schooling established the framework for his remarkable career as a musician and composer. His background in a musical family, his numerous musical inspirations, and his study at some of the finest music schools in the UK all led to his distinct creative vision and his enduring effect on the world of music.

Chapter 2: Jazz and Jazz-Rock Fusion Maestro - Notable Works, Influence, and Impact on his Musical Journey

Sir Karl Jenkins is a Welsh composer and performer who has had a considerable effect on the world of music, notably in the disciplines of classical, jazz, and jazz-rock fusion.

Throughout his career, he has explored a broad variety of musical styles and genres, infusing aspects of jazz into many of his pieces. This has resulted in some of his most memorable and highly lauded compositions and has solidified his status as one of the most original and versatile composers of our day.

Jenkins' interest in jazz started early in his career, when he performed as a session musician with numerous jazz ensembles and performers. He was notably inspired by the music of Miles Davis, John Coltrane, and other jazz greats of the 1960s and 1970s.

This exposure to the jazz environment helped to mold his approach to composition, as he started to experiment with mixing jazz harmonies and rhythms into his classical compositions. As his career evolved, Jenkins became more active in the jazz and jazz-rock movements, both as a musician and as a writer.

He performed with a number of jazz ensembles, notably the jazz-rock fusion group Nucleus, and collaborated with a range of jazz performers and producers. This experience provided him with a strong grasp of the genre and enabled him to explore new and unique methods of infusing jazz into his music.

Jenkins' jazz-influenced compositions are some of his most popular and highly regarded pieces. One of his early jazz-inspired songs was on the 1980 album "Faces of Jazz", which was a collaboration with the jazz trio Soft Machine. This CD was well-received and demonstrated Jenkins' ability to merge jazz and classical music in a new and captivating manner.

Another significant work in this manner is "Adiemus", a set of compositions that Jenkins created in the 1990s. These songs have elaborate vocal arrangements and integrate aspects of jazz, world music, and classical music. The music is marked by its intricate rhythms and harmonies and has become one of Jenkins' defining compositions.

Jenkins' jazz and jazz-rock fusion pieces are also known for their use of electronic instruments. He typically integrates synthesizers, drum machines, and other electronic instruments into his music, which gives it a distinct and contemporary vibe.

Jazz has had a major impact on Jenkins' music, both in terms of its style and its ideology. Jenkins has claimed that he is attracted to jazz because of its focus on improvisation and spontaneity, which he feels are key qualities of music-making.

He has also remarked on the significance of rhythm in jazz and how it has encouraged him to explore new and unique rhythmic patterns in his own work. Incorporating jazz into his work has also helped Jenkins break down boundaries across genres and produce music that is both accessible and unique.

His jazz-influenced pieces have been successful with audiences throughout the globe and have contributed to widening the bounds of classical music. Jenkins' contributions to jazz and jazz-rock fusion have not just been restricted to his own compositions but also to his collaborations with other musicians.

One famous collaboration was his work with the British jazz-rock fusion band Nucleus. Jenkins performed keyboards for the band, and his efforts contributed to creating a distinctive and varied sound that mixed jazz, rock, and classical music.

In addition to his work with Nucleus, Jenkins has worked with a number of other jazz performers and producers. He has collaborated with the jazz singer Cleo Laine as well as the jazz drummer Kenny Wheeler. These partnerships have enabled Jenkins to explore fresh and unique methods of mixing jazz into his work and have helped to extend his musical horizons.

One of the fundamental components of Jenkins' jazz-inspired pieces is his use of rhythm. Jenkins has remarked on the significance of rhythm in jazz and how it has inspired his own approach to music-making. He has worked with a broad spectrum of rhythmic patterns, from intricate time signatures to unorthodox accents and syncopations.

This experimentation has resulted in some of his most memorable and original pieces and has served to separate his work from that of other composers. Jenkins' jazz-inspired tunes have also been lauded for their accessibility.

While jazz may often be viewed as a specialist genre, Jenkins' music has wide appeal and has been welcomed by listeners throughout the globe. His compositions generally have memorable melodies and appealing rhythms, which make them easy to listen to and admire.

This accessibility has helped to promote jazz to a larger audience and has helped to break down boundaries across genres. Another noticeable characteristic of Jenkins' jazz-inspired pieces is his use of vocal music.

Jenkins has composed numerous songs that utilize sophisticated vocal arrangements, typically performed by huge choirs or vocal groups. These pieces, such as "Adiemus" and "The Armed Man", merge elements of classical and world music with jazz harmonies and rhythms, producing a distinctive and powerful sound.

Jenkins has claimed that he views the voice as another instrument in his work and that he likes experimenting with various vocal methods and textures. He has also remarked on the significance of language in vocal music and how he frequently takes inspiration from poetry and other literary works.

Jenkins' passion for vocal music has led to collaborations with a number of prominent singers and vocal ensembles. He has collaborated with the famed Welsh choir, Only Men Aloud, as well as the vocal group, The Sixteen.

These partnerships have enabled him to produce compositions that are both musically difficult and emotionally resonant. Jenkins has regularly integrated synthesizers, drum machines, and other electronic instruments into his works, giving them a current and unique feel.

This usage of electronic instrumentation has helped to bridge the gap between classical and jazz music and has helped to develop a new and interesting sub-genre called jazz-rock fusion. Jenkins' jazz-inspired works have also been lauded for their use of improvisation.

While his pieces are painstakingly prepared and arranged, they typically incorporate improvised solos by individual performers, bringing an element of spontaneity and energy to the performances.

This improvisation is a trademark of jazz music, and Jenkins' inclusion of it into his songs has served to further blur the distinctions between genres.

In conclusion, Karl Jenkins' contributions to the world of jazz and jazz-rock fusion are both substantial and diverse. His unique approach to composition, which integrates elements of classical, jazz, and world music, has developed a body of work that is both inventive and accessible.

His collaborations with other jazz artists, his experiments with rhythm and vocal music, and his use of electronic instruments have contributed to broadening the frontiers of jazz and developing a new and intriguing sub-genre of jazz-rock fusion.

Chapter 3: From Modern Rhythms to Timeless Melodies- Jenkins' Remarkable Journey into Classical Music

Sir Karl Jenkins is a highly acclaimed and versatile composer who has made substantial contributions to both jazz and classical music. Although he started his career in the field of jazz, Jenkins' shift to classical music composition has been remarkable.

He has created a number of notable works in the classical genre and has cooperated with some of the world's most recognized orchestras and performers.One of Jenkins' most renowned compositions in the classical genre is "The Armed Man: A Mass for Peace".

This choral composition was commissioned by the Royal Armouries Museum in Leeds, England, to welcome the new century. The work blends conventional parts of the Catholic Mass with a range of other influences, including folk music and jazz.

The outcome is a powerful and poignant composition that has been performed by choirs and orchestras all across the globe.

Another significant piece by Jenkins is his "Requiem". This composition was produced in commemoration of his father and mixes elements of classical music with Welsh traditional music. The work is arranged for a big orchestra, choir, and soloists and is distinguished by its haunting melodies and evocative harmonies.

Jenkins has also composed a variety of concerti for other instruments, including the saxophone, cello, and euphonium. These pieces have been performed by some of the world's best-known soloists and have earned Jenkins a reputation as a master of the concerto form.

In addition to his own works, Jenkins has worked with a number of other classical performers and organizations. He has composed pieces for the BBC National Orchestra of Wales, the London Symphony Orchestra, and the Kirov Orchestra, among others.

He has also cooperated with performers such as violinist Tasmin Little and cellist Julian Lloyd Webber.One of the trademarks of Jenkins' classical music works is his use of melody.

His songs are marked by distinctive and lyrical melodies that typically take influence from a range of genres, including folk music and jazz. Jenkins has also been recognized for his use of harmony and orchestration, which are both original and successful.

Jenkins' works in the classical form are especially remarkable for their emotional depth and intricacy. He has created works that explore a broad variety of subjects and emotions, from the power of love and the beauty of nature to the sorrow of war and the battle for peace.

His ability to compose music that is both musically advanced and emotionally compelling has gained him a passionate following among classical music aficionados throughout the globe.

Sir Karl Jenkins' contributions to the realm of classical music have been enormous and lasting. His distinctive approach, which integrates elements of classical, folk, and jazz music, has developed a collection of work that is both inventive and accessible.

His partnerships with other classical performers and groups have served to widen the reach of his music, and his ability to compose emotionally compelling compositions has gained him a committed audience.

In addition to his well-known compositions in the classical genre, Jenkins has also made substantial contributions to other fields of music, including cinema soundtracks and television themes.

He has created music for various films, including "The Journey" and "Adiemus Colores". His music has also been featured in a number of television series, including the BBC's "The Human Planet" and "The World's Most Dangerous Roads".

One of the things that makes Jenkins' classical works distinct is his desire to explore other musical genres and traditions. He has taken influence from a broad array of sources, including world music, jazz, and even electronic dance music.

This eagerness to explore new musical frontiers has served to keep Jenkins' work fresh and fascinating and has helped to push the bounds of classical music.

Jenkins' devotion to social justice and human rights has also had a key impact on his classical works. Many of his works, like "The Armed Man" and "Requiem", explore themes of war, violence, and the quest for peace. He has also created music that celebrates the beauty of nature and the strength of love, like his "Stella Natalis" and "Gloria" pieces.

Another characteristic of Jenkins' classical pieces that sets them apart is his use of voice music. He has produced a variety of choral works that contain elaborate vocal harmonies and textures and are frequently performed by huge choirs or vocal groups.

His "The Peacemakers" composition, for example, has sections for choir, soloists, and a narrator and relies on a number of diverse musical genres and traditions.

Jenkins' devotion to education and outreach has also had a key impact on his classical music works. He has been engaged in a variety of programs meant to expose classical music to larger audiences, including the "Classic FM Hall of Fame" project, which allows listeners to vote for their favorite classical pieces. He has also been active in music education efforts, including seminars and masterclasses for young musicians.

It is worth mentioning that Jenkins' contributions to the classical music genre have not gone forgotten. He has earned various prizes and distinctions during his career, including a knighthood in 2015 for his contributions to music.

He has also been given the CBE (Commander of the Order of the British Empire) and the OBE (Officer of the Order of the British Empire) for his services to music.

Jenkins has also worked with some of the greatest names in classical music, including cellist Julian Lloyd Webber, vocalist Kiri Te Kanawa, and conductor Sir Simon Rattle. He has created music for significant events like the Olympic Games, notably the music for the opening and closing ceremonies of the 2004 Athens Olympics and the 2012 London Olympics.

In addition to his collaborations with other musicians and composers, Jenkins has also formed various musical groupings and organizations. He developed the Adiemus project in 1994, which mixes classical music with world music influences and incorporates the unusual voice of Miriam Stockley. He has also created the Karl

Jenkins Music Award, which is presented yearly to a young artist or group of musicians to assist their musical growth.

Sir Karl Jenkins' contributions to the classical music field are wide and far-reaching. His distinctive approach, which mixes classical, world music, and other inspirations, has developed a body of work that is both accessible and original.

His devotion to social justice and human rights has also made him a significant figure in the classical music world and has helped to produce works that are both musically and emotionally compelling.

Chapter 4: Adiemus: A Harmonious Odyssey of World Music Fusion and Jenkins' Creative Prowess

Adiemus is a unique and intriguing musical concept that demonstrates the harmonic synthesis of global music components with classical and modern influences. The brainchild of Welsh composer Karl Jenkins, Adiemus has garnered worldwide fame and praise for its unique sound and creative brilliance.

Through a mix of compelling vocal performances, sophisticated orchestral arrangements, and a celebration of many musical traditions, Jenkins has constructed a really amazing musical adventure.

Jenkins' artistic talent certainly shows through in Adiemus, which was initially revealed to the public in 1994 with the release of the album "Adiemus: Songs of Sanctuary."

The project's name, "Adiemus," is a phrase devised by Jenkins himself and carries no specific significance. It expresses the notion of a global language spoken via music, transcending cultural barriers and communicating with listeners on a deep emotional level.

At the core of Adiemus are the amazing vocal performances that have become associated with the project. Jenkins used a group of exceptional singers, known as the Adiemus Singers, to bring his works to life.

Their voices, frequently singing in imagined languages and with elaborate vocal techniques, function as instruments in their own right, imparting an ethereal and otherworldly aspect to the music.

One of the most intriguing qualities of Adiemus is the seamless merging of global music components from many nations and traditions. Jenkins takes inspiration from a broad variety of musical forms, including African, Celtic, Aboriginal, and Eastern influences.

By mixing these disparate themes with classical and modern orchestration, he produces a beautiful combination that is both approachable and emotionally touching.

The orchestral arrangements of Adiemus are painstakingly produced, displaying Jenkins' extraordinary mastery over composition and his ability to elicit a broad variety of emotions.

The music generally incorporates lush string sections, strong brass arrangements, and rhythmic percussion, all working together to create a rich and layered musical world. The employment of unorthodox instruments, such as the duduk, didgeridoo, and Japanese taiko drums, further strengthens the worldwide tapestry of sound.

Jenkins' creative skill is obvious in his ability to take difficult musical concepts and convey them in a manner that connects with a large audience. The songs of Adiemus are frequently immediately memorable, with a feeling of grandeur and cinematic beauty.

The song has been utilized in several film, television, and commercial productions, further reinforcing its global popularity.

Beyond its musical accomplishments, Adiemus conveys a feeling of solidarity and appreciation for variety. By combining components from diverse cultures, Jenkins displays the potential of music to transcend linguistic and cultural boundaries, generating a feeling of common humanity.

The initiative serves as a reminder of the global language of music and its capacity to inspire emotions and unite people from all walks of life.

Adiemus shines as a monument to Karl Jenkins' outstanding creative skill. Through his original blend of world music, classical composition, and modern inspirations, Jenkins has constructed a musical journey that captivates and inspires audiences worldwide.

Adiemus is a hymn to the power of music, highlighting the harmonizing beauty that may be produced when various traditions join together in a symphony of sound.

Adiemus continues to grow and expand with succeeding albums, each presenting a distinct examination of musical topics and cultural influences.

Jenkins recorded numerous albums under the Adiemus moniker, including "Adiemus II: Cantata Mundi," "Adiemus III: Dances of Time," and "Adiemus IV: The Eternal Knot," among others. Each album retains the characteristic Adiemus sound while delving into new territory and musical soundscapes.

The success of Adiemus may be traced to Jenkins' ability to achieve a careful balance between familiarity and novelty. While based in classical and choral traditions, the music transcends classification, bringing a new and modern perspective to these genres.

Jenkins' works smoothly merge classical melodies with current production methods, adding electronic components, delicate rhythms, and ambient soundscapes. This mix offers a compelling auditory experience that appeals to both classical lovers and those seeking something fresh and intriguing.

Another striking component of Jenkins' creative approach is his use of the human voice as a major instrument. The Adiemus Singers, with their strong and evocative vocal performances, play a crucial role in communicating the emotional depth of the song.

Through sophisticated vocal harmonies, soaring melodies, and rhythmic chants, they become conduits for the global language of music, conveying a spectrum of emotions that transcend linguistic borders.

Jenkins' talent as a composer goes beyond his work with Adiemus. He has created several classical pieces, orchestral suites, cinema music, and even a Requiem that have gained critical praise.

His works generally integrate standard Western classical components with inspirations from diverse cultural traditions, resulting in a unique and engaging musical language.

The significance of Adiemus stretches well beyond the sphere of recorded music. The project has been performed live by orchestras and choirs across the globe, impressing audiences with its immersive and transcendent characteristics.

Jenkins' ability to smoothly combine varied musical parts into his pieces enables performers to add their own interpretations, thus improving the live experience.

Adiemus serves as a testimony to the ability of music to create cultural understanding and respect. By taking inspiration from numerous musical traditions, Jenkins inspires listeners to enjoy the beauty of other cultures and embrace a feeling of oneness through song.

In a world frequently separated by borders and divisions, Adiemus gives a reminder of our common humanity and the possibility for reconciliation when we honor our joint past.

Karl Jenkins' artistic brilliance shines brilliantly through his work on Adiemus. His ability to weave together a tapestry of global music influences, classical grandeur, and modern invention displays a depth of musical knowledge and a drive to push creative frontiers. Adiemus serves as a tribute to Jenkins' creative vision and his ability to produce music that connects strongly with listeners worldwide.

In conclusion, Adiemus is not only a harmonic adventure of global music fusion but also a testimonial to Karl Jenkins' creative brilliance. Through the merging of varied musical influences, excellent orchestration, and engaging vocal performances, Jenkins produces a musical experience that transcends borders and speaks to the universal language of music.

Adiemus serves as a tribute to the power of creative vision, cultural appreciation, and the transformational character of music itself.

Chapter 5: Personal Life, Philanthropy and Activism

Sir Karl Jenkins' personal life is defined by a great devotion to charity and social activity. He is noted not just for his musical achievements but also for his participation in a range of philanthropic causes.

Jenkins has been open about his ideas about the ability of music to promote social change and bring people together across cultural and political barriers. He has cooperated with several groups to assist with social and environmental problems and has utilized his music to generate awareness and funding for different humanitarian efforts.

One of the issues closest to Jenkins' heart is music education. He has long been an advocate for the value of music in schools and has worked with groups such as Music for Youth and the National Youth Music Theatre to promote music education and give young people chances to connect with music.

Jenkins has also been active with a variety of groups focusing on social justice and human rights. He has worked with Amnesty International and other groups to raise awareness of problems such as torture, human trafficking, and the plight of refugees.
Jenkins' charity involvement spans beyond music and human rights. He has also been concerned with environmental concerns, working

with groups such as the World Wildlife Fund to raise awareness of the consequences of climate change and promote conservation initiatives.

In addition to his work with humanitarian organizations, Jenkins has also been active with several cultural institutions and events. He has served as composer-in-residence at the London Symphony Orchestra and the Royal Welsh College of Music and Drama and has worked with festivals such as the Proms and the Edinburgh Festival.

Sir Karl Jenkins' engagement with many organizations and issues demonstrates his dedication to utilizing music as a vehicle for social change and to promoting the principles of inclusion and empathy across cultures.

His humanitarian endeavors and social activity have made him not just a distinguished composer and conductor but also a recognized and important voice in the larger cultural and political realms.

Jenkins' charitable and social activities have expanded beyond his work with particular organizations. He has utilized his music to raise awareness of numerous topics and promote themes of peace, togetherness, and understanding.

One famous example of this is the Adicmus project, which was created as a celebration of the human voice and of the power of music to bring people together across cultural and language differences.

The music of Adiemus draws on a range of global music traditions, including African and Latin American rhythms, Indian vocal methods, and European choir genres, and mixes them with Jenkins' particular musical sensibility to produce a sound that is both original and emotionally touching.

Through Adiemus and other initiatives, Jenkins has worked to promote a message of cultural interchange and mutual respect, stressing the richness and variety of the world's musical traditions and underscoring the need to recognize and appreciate our common humanity.

Jenkins' engagement with humanitarian organizations has also had a direct influence on people's lives. He has collaborated with groups such as the charity Mary's Meals, which offers food and education to children in some of the world's poorest regions, and has used his songs to collect donations for their work.

In addition to his generosity and social activity, Jenkins has also been acknowledged for his contributions to the world of music. He has been granted various honors and prizes, including a knighthood in 2015, and his music has been performed by some of the world's greatest orchestras and groups.
Overall, Sir Karl Jenkins' life and work are defined by a profound dedication to utilizing music as an instrument for social change and

to promoting the principles of inclusion, empathy, and understanding across cultures.

Through his music and his generosity, he has had a huge effect on the globe and has encouraged many people to utilize their own skills and resources to make a good change in the world.

Chapter 6: Legacy and Transformative Impact of Sir Karl Jenkins On Music

Sir Karl Jenkins is a Welsh composer and performer who has had a considerable effect on modern music. With a career spanning over four decades, Jenkins has developed a significant body of work that has garnered him several honors and prizes, including two Ivor Novello prizes, a Grammy Award, and a CBE from Queen Elizabeth II.

Jenkins' effect on current music may be traced to his distinctive approach that integrates many musical genres, including classical, jazz, and world music. He has also combined aspects of traditional Welsh music into his works, producing a sound that is unique and unmistakable.

One of Jenkins' most notable contributions to current music is his founding of the Adiemus project. Adiemus is a series of CDs that offer a unique combination of classical and world music, with vocals sung in a fictional language devised by Jenkins.

The Adiemus project has been tremendously popular, with millions of recordings sold globally. In addition to his work with Adiemus, Jenkins has also created other choral works, notably The Armed Man: A Mass for Peace, which has become one of the most performed pieces of classical music in recent years.

The work was initially performed in 2000 and has subsequently been played by various orchestras and choirs throughout the globe. The Armed Man has also been utilized in various film soundtracks, including The Hobbit: The Battle of the Five Armies.

Jenkins' cultural effect and legacy may be observed in his contributions to modern music as well as his role as an advocate for Welsh music and culture. His works have been played at prominent events such as the opening ceremony of the 2004 Summer Olympics in Athens, Greece, and the 2014 Commonwealth Games in Glasgow, Scotland.

Jenkins has also been an advocate for music education and has worked with various groups to promote music education in schools. He has developed the Karl Jenkins Music Award, which is granted annually to a talented young musician in Wales.

Sir Karl Jenkins' influence and effect on current music are enormous. His distinctive style and combination of numerous musical genres have gained him a worldwide audience, and his contributions to choral music, notably The Armed Man, have established his position in classical music history.

Sir Karl Jenkins' effect on current music goes beyond his own pieces. He has also worked with various musicians, including Sting, Bryn Terfel, and Plácido Domingo.

In 2014, he joined with the London Symphony Orchestra and the London Philharmonic Choir to produce The Peacemakers, a choral piece that commemorates the lives of outstanding peacemakers throughout history.

Jenkins' music has been utilized in different types of media, including cinema, television, and video games. His composition "Palladio" was utilized in the famous computer game Civilization IV, and his music has been included in films such as The Revenant, The Dark Knight, and The Kingsman.

In addition to his musical talents, Jenkins has also been honored for his contributions to Welsh culture. In 2004, he was granted the Glyndwr Award for his contribution to the arts in Wales, and in 2015, he was admitted into the Gorsedd of Bards, a Welsh cultural institution that acknowledges persons who have made important contributions to Welsh language, literature, and culture.

Jenkins' legacy also includes his position as a mentor and inspiration to future artists. He has been known to work closely with new composers and performers, giving them direction and encouragement to help them improve their art.

Many of these artists have gone on to achieve their own success, recognizing Jenkins as a big influence on their work. Another notable feature of Jenkins' effect on current music is his use of music as a medium for conveying social and political agendas.

In The Armed Man: A Mass for Peace, he explores issues of war, conflict, and reconciliation. The composition contains passages from numerous religious and cultural traditions, highlighting the universality of these ideas. Jenkins has also been active in numerous humanitarian initiatives, utilizing his songs to promote awareness and donations for different organizations.

He has partnered with groups like Save the Children and the British Red Cross to arrange benefit performances and records, collecting millions of dollars for philanthropic causes.

In addition to his work in music education, Jenkins has also been a prominent proponent of diversity in the arts. He has spoken out against prejudice and discrimination in the music business, pushing for better representation and opportunity for musicians from varied backgrounds.

Jenkins' effect on current music is also evident in the various prizes and distinctions he has earned. In addition to his Ivor Novello and Grammy Awards, he has been given the Queen's Medal for Music and the Classical BRIT Award for Composer of the Year.

He was also given a Knight Bachelor in the 2015 New Year's Honors for his contributions to music.

In conclusion, Sir Karl Jenkins' legacy and effect on current music are varied and far-reaching. His distinctive style, support for music education and diversity, and use of music for social and political causes have made him an important figure in the world of music.

His impact is seen not just through his own compositions but also through the numerous musicians and artists he has inspired and mentored.

Chapter 7: The Lookalike Saga

On May 10, 2023, King Charles III of the United Kingdom culminated in a ceremony at Westminster Abbey. The event was attended by numerous prominent numbers from around the world, including celebrities, politicians, and members of the royal family.

One of the guests at the coronation was Sir Karl Jenkins, a Welsh musician and captain. Jenkins is a well- known presence in the classical music world, and his work has been performed by some of the world's top symphonies. He's also a philanthropist of the Order of the British Empire.

Jenkins sat in the frontal row of the monastery for the coronation, and he was readily visible on TV footage of the form. Still, multitudinous observers were quick to observe that Jenkins had a significant likeness to Meghan Markle, the Duchess of Sussex.

Markle is a former American actress who married Prince Harry, Duke of Sussex, in 2018. She has been a polarizing figure since joining the royal family, and she and Harry have recently stepped back from their formal commitments.

The parallels between Jenkins and Markle were so astonishing that some observers began to presume that Markle had disguised herself as Jenkins in order to attend the coronation without being detected.

This proposition was fleetly picked up by the media, and it soon became a hot topic of discussion on social media. Of course, there's no substantiation to confirm the allegation that Markle disguised herself as Jenkins.

Jenkins himself has rejected the claim, and there's no reason to assume that he'd lie about commodities like this. It appears more likely that the similarity between Jenkins and Markle is purely a coexistence. Both people are of mixed heritage, and they both share analogous facial characteristics.

It's also worth considering that Jenkins is an addict of Markle, and he has spoken largely of her in the history. The conspiracy proposition linking Jenkins and Markle has been a source of entertainment for numerous people.

Still, it has also been terrible for Jenkins, who has been indicted of being a fabricator and a fake. Jenkins has said that he's" disappointed" by the way in which he has been treated, and he has prayed people to stop propagating the conspiracy proposition. He has also said that he's" proud" to be a British citizen and that he's happy" to have attended the coronation.

Printed in Great Britain
by Amazon

49107749R00030